Original title:
Beneath the Roof of Hope

Copyright © 2025 Creative Arts Management OÜ
All rights reserved.

Author: Hugo Fitzgerald
ISBN HARDBACK: 978-1-80587-201-6
ISBN PAPERBACK: 978-1-80587-671-7

Where Every Tear Can Spark a Flame

In a world where water flows,
Sometimes it leads to quirky shows.
You cry a bit, then laugh and grin,
Turning mishaps into wins.

A slip on ice, a sudden splash,
We turn our woes to comic trash.
With each small tear, a chuckle blooms,
Creating joy in crowded rooms.

The Branches of Promise and Possibility

Underneath a sprawling tree,
The squirrels plot and giggle with glee.
For every nut they've lost in flight,
They find a new one, oh what a sight!

Promises branch out every day,
Like limbs so sturdy, come what may.
Fruits of laughter grow so sweet,
A chance to dance on life's repeat.

A Voyage into the Unseen Future

Set sail on ships of cereal bowls,
With milk as waves, we chase our goals.
The future glimmers like a spark,
Even if it feels quite dark.

With spoons as oars, we paddle fast,
Through silly storms, we're unsurpassed.
Wherever we roam, be it near or far,
The laughter's our bright guiding star.

The Cradle of Compassion and Kindness

In a cozy nook where giggles abide,
Hugs and laughter are the joyful tide.
A simple smile, a quirky dance,
In this haven, we take a chance.

With kindness cradled soft and warm,
We weather storms and quit the norm.
Together we rise, we stumble, we play,
In delightful antics, we find our way.

Echoes of Light in Dusk's Lullaby

In the evening glow, laughter flies,
Cats dance like stars in the moonlit skies.
Shadows tickle each corner of fun,
While dreams giggle softly, one by one.

Silly whispers float on the breeze,
Giggling ghosts dance among the trees.
A tickle here, a poke in the night,
As stars play tag in the fading light.

Where the Soul Finds Its Wings

In a closet full of mismatched socks,
A secret hideaway amidst the clocks.
Here, the silly giggles take their flight,
As we dodge the shadows, oh what a sight!

Balloons float high with a cheerful grin,
Chasing worries as they spin and spin.
In each tug of laughter, we find a way,
To dance through troubles that might delay.

Light Breaking Through the Canopy of Shadows

With sunbeams sneaking through leafy hats,
Chasing away the grumpiest cats.
Each ray a jester, bright and bold,
Turning shadows into stories told.

Banana peels slip on a winter's chill,
As light bursts forth and gives us a thrill.
In this patchwork quilt of silly delight,
We gather our dreams, ready for flight.

The Nest of Dreams and Desires

A nest is built of wishes and cheer,
With a side of giggles and a splash of beer.
Each feather added brings a smile,
As we dream out loud and stay awhile.

With chuckles echoing under the stars,
And dancing fireflies in tiny jars.
We'll craft our world with a twinkle and wink,
In this nest of dreams, let's laugh and think.

The Pulse of Tomorrow in a Waking Dream

In a dream where slippers dance,
And cats wear hats that sing,
The alarm clock joins the prance,
As toast begins to spring.

Butterflies are wearing ties,
While muffins boast a grin,
A world where rubber chickens fly,
As laughter twirls in spin.

The sun has hobbies, don't you see?
It juggles rays all day,
While shadows shout with glee,
In a wacky ballet.

So hold on tight to whimsy's thread,
In this dull life, avoid the frown.
Tomorrow's pulse is full of tread,
With jokes that wear a crown.

In the Whispering Breeze of Change

A breeze carries ticklish notes,
That make the tulips giggle,
While zany squirrels learn to float,
In a dance that steals the wiggle.

Pigeons wear aviator shades,
As they strut their finest flair,
The wind tells tales of charades,
With tumbleweeds that dare.

Kites are keeling, tickled skies,
As clouds play peek-a-boo,
While laughter flutters, rarely lies,
In a breeze, all fun is true.

So let the whispers melt your cares,
In this playful, wicked range,
With every twist, a joke ensnares,
In the breeze where dreams arrange.

Shadows that Illuminate the Heart

Even shadows like to play,
In the corners of the room,
They're singing songs of yesterday,
With a hint of comic gloom.

A lamp is grinning, light on tilt,
As shadows jump for joy,
It spills the beans, no need for guilt,
While giggles start to buoy.

They dance upon the wall with flair,
Making faces, mischief shared,
In the laughter, none despair,
As night laughs, fully prepared.

So embrace the shade as it glows,
And let your heart take part,
In this world where humor flows,
From shadows that gently chart.

A Symphony of Light in the Dark

In the dark, where giggles swell,
And glow worms form a band,
They play a tune, oh what a spell,
As laughter takes a stand.

The moon is a cheeky conductor,
With stars as sparkling clowns,
They jive and twirl, a night of grandeur,
In mischievous gowns.

Crickets harmonize in sync,
While fireflies strut their stuff,
A symphony that's hard to think,
With humor, never tough.

So close your eyes, let music spark,
In this festive, jovial arc,
Join the growth, a quirky lark,
In a symphony where dreams embark.

Shadows of Tomorrow's Light

In a world where things seem bright,
Shadows dance, they take their flight.
Pigeons plot in covert schemes,
While squirrels waltz in silly dreams.

Jellybeans rain from the sky,
While UFOs dance, oh my!
Laughter echoes in the air,
As silly hats are worn with flair.

Optimism wears striped socks,
Bouncing high, it never knocks.
With a wink and a goofy grin,
Tomorrow's light is sure to win!

So let's flip pancakes on the lawn,
And sing to the moon till the break of dawn.
For in this goofy, bright delight,
We'll find our way to future's light.

Embracing Stars in Quiet Nights

Under a blanket of shimmering fun,
Stars giggle and twinkle, one by one.
Never a moment of silence here,
As coyotes join in, giving a cheer.

Marshmallows grow legs and dance around,
While crickets play a lively sound.
Bugs having parties quite absurd,
They take turns with humor unheard.

Wishes fly like kites in the breeze,
In a world where nothing's a tease.
Laughter soars, chasing the night,
As dreams take wing and soar in flight.

So let's toast to the stars so bright,
With chocolate fountains pure delight.
In the silliness, our hearts take flight,
Embracing magic through the night.

The Sanctuary of Unspoken Dreams

In a corner where whispers curl,
Lies a sanctuary of every whirl.
Paper cranes are plotting their flight,
While ice cream castles shine so bright.

Tickle fights with shadows at play,
As laughter echoes, come what may.
Doodles on the wall, a map unclear,
Leading us to dreams held dear.

Giggles bloom like flowers in spring,
In this quiet place where gnomes sing.
Candles flicker without a care,
As dreams do pirouettes in the air.

So let us paint the walls with cheer,
And fill the silence with giggles near.
In this haven of visions so grand,
Unspoken dreams take a stand.

A Haven for the Longing Heart

In a garden where giggles sprout,
You'll find the heart dancing about.
With daffodils wearing silly hats,
And butterflies hosting tea for cats.

Lemonade fountains with flavors so odd,
As fireflies twinkle, giving a nod.
Balloons shaped like fish swim the sky,
While rain clouds wear smiles, oh my!

With dreams wrapped in candy-coated dreams,
Every laugh is better than it seems.
In a hammock, we swing and sway,
Chasing our worries far away.

So raise a toast with jelly shots,
In this haven, we'll tie our knots.
For in this joy, we find our song,
Where longing hearts truly belong.

The Heart's Hidden Oasis

In a place where dreams wear socks,
And giggles dance with silly rocks,
Marshmallow clouds take jellybeans,
As laughter floats on sunny streams.

A cactus tried to tell a joke,
But ended up with sunburnt smoke,
The trees wear hats, a culture clash,
While butterflies make quite a splash.

With lemonade that sparkles bright,
And dancing squirrels that feel just right,
A harmony of silly tunes,
As we chase shadows with bright balloons.

So come and join this merry spree,
Where whimsy reigns, and hearts feel free,
In this oasis full of cheer,
We'll laugh our way till night draws near.

Echoes of Forgotten Aspirations

Where old dreams lie beneath the bed,
With crumpled notes the cat has fed,
A bicycle without a tire,
Joins a game of hide-and-fire.

With ghosts of goals that wear a grin,
Dancing thin air, they draw us in,
They whisper secrets, half-formed schemes,
While raindrops play on dusty beams.

A rubber duck with a feathered hat,
Tells old tales of a brave old cat,
Who thought he'd soar like a seagull,
But landed well, just to be full.

So let's toast marshmallows to the past,
With gooey smiles that seem to last,
For in the echoes, we still find,
The wacky dreams we left behind.

Beneath Canopies of Possibility

In gardens where the daisies dance,
A bumblebee asks if there's a chance,
To wear a coat of bright mint green,
And throw a party, all unseen.

The wind must think it's quite the tease,
With voices swirling through the trees,
It tickles leaves, it plays a tune,
Makes shadows play like a cartoon.

A snail that dreams of racing fast,
Wears shades to hide his slow contrast,
While ladybugs hum, twirl and sway,
In a world that's quirky every day.

So let's create with silly flair,
In this garden with vibrant air,
For wonders bloom, day after day,
In canopies where laughter plays.

Among the Stars of Belief

In a sky where wishes sometimes leap,
And twinkling stars perform a sweep,
A cow with shades rides on a comet,
Spreading joy like a warm sonnet.

The moon wears socks that don't quite match,
As comets plot their cheeky hatch,
A giggle bounces off the night,
With planets winking, feels just right.

Dreamers gather in space cafes,
Sharing laughter in strange ways,
With cups of stardust, snacks of light,
They toast to hopes that feel so bright.

So let us dance among the beams,
And chase our wildest, wackiest dreams,
For among the stars, we just might find,
The joy of living, intertwined.

Reflections in the Reservoir of Dreams

In a pond where frogs wear crowns,
They debate the best of towns.
One claims a fly is rare as gold,
While others just feel very bold.

Moonbeams whisper missed chances,
As turtles practice fancy dances.
With every splash, they sing and laugh,
Creating ripples on the path.

These dreams take shape in wobbly towers,
Stacked high with mismatched flower hours.
Who knew a snail could lead a race,
While ducks just waddle with grace?

In laughter, hopes play hide and seek,
As daisies share their secrets, unique.
A frog leaps high, a brave little knight,
In the dreamland, everything feels right.

The Bridge Above the Chasm of Doubt

Across the gap, a rubber band,
Holds dreams that float like grains of sand.
Yet pigeons plot to steal a snack,
While squirrels conspire at the back.

A comedian swings on vines of trust,
Saying, "Don't tread here, or bust!"
With a wink and a nudge, they all agree,
That laughter is the key, you see.

Balancing act of hopes and fears,
Juggling dreams while dodging jeers.
But in the end, it's all a joke,
As laughter rings and doubts just choke.

So take a step, embrace the tease,
For giggles float on gentle breeze.
A bridge of joy, constructed bright,
Will guide us through the silliest night.

Threads of Silver in the Fabric of Night

Stars like buttons in a quilt,
Dancing 'round where laughter's built.
A cat takes flight on a milky cloud,
While mice throw parties, all quite loud.

With owls in top hats sipping tea,
They toast to dreams that could never be.
Each thread tells tales of fabled lore,
Spun with humor, who could ask for more?

The moon's a disco ball, it's said,
Where shadows dance and fears are shed.
Under this cover of silvery light,
Everything seems just hilariously right.

So wrap yourself in dreams tonight,
Let silly hopes take daring flight.
For within this fabric, laughter lies,
In the winks and giggles of starry skies.

The Sewn Together Pieces of Tomorrow

With patches stitched from yesterdays,
Dreams fold up in quirky ways.
A hat made of wishes, oh so bright,
Dances in the wind, such a sight!

Socks mismatched tell a story true,
Of all the goofy things we do.
A kite made from newspaper clippings,
Soars high with laughter, no slipping.

Each seam a memory, vivid and bold,
Of gaffes and giggles, and tales retold.
A quilt of moments, stitched by fate,
Where joy unravels, never too late.

So here's to tomorrow, come what may,
With threads of fun that brightly play.
In this patchwork, let joy reside,
As we navigate the wild ride.

When Hearts Speak the Language of Strength

In a room where laughter plays,
Hearts chat in silly ways,
Strength comes from goofy fable,
Breaking bread and maybe a table.

We dance like penguins on ice,
Each misstep is worth the price,
With strength wrapped in humor's fold,
Tales of bravery, freshly told.

A toaster leaps, we cheer and shout,
It pops, and crumbs are all about,
In this chaos, we find our might,
As jokes ignite the starry night.

When hearts collide with glee and cheer,
Strength blooms, and shadows disappear,
In laughter's arms, we're never weak,
Through humor's lens, we proudly speak.

The Gathering of Light and Shadow

In the alley where shadows play,
Light winks in a cheeky way,
A party of flickers, oh so bright,
Inviting all to join the plight.

A lamp jumped in, a silly sight,
Together, they dance in the night,
Light and shadow, a comical pair,
Chasing each other everywhere.

As dusk falls with a gentle sway,
The heart of laughter leads the way,
A giggle here, a chuckle there,
They craft the night with utmost care.

In this gathering, joy's the creed,
Companions sure, with laughter freed,
For even shadows yearn for light,
Together they share the whimsical night.

Rustling Leaves of Forgotten Hopes

Leaves chatter like gossips in line,
What happened when dreams were divine?
Forgotten hopes in crispy attire,
Whisper stories that never tire.

A twig dances, declaring a show,
While acorns giggle down below,
These rustling leaves create a din,
Saying, 'Who knows where to begin?'

In this woodland, dreams flip and flop,
Some take a leap, some just stop,
Yet in their rustle lies a jest,
That life is best when we're a mess.

So we gather hopes like socks from a drawer,
Laughing loudly, forever wanting more,
With leaves a-swaying, our hearts proclaim,
In this chaos, we're all the same.

In the Warmth of Every Breath

Each breath we take is a funny cheer,
Like bubbles popping, bright and clear,
In warmth we find our laughter's glow,
As joy expands, like dough in flow.

With morning's giggle, the sun peeks through,
Tickling noses, the laughter grew,
In this cuddle of vibrant air,
We breathe in jokes without a care.

As bedtime whispers, dreams take flight,
While pillows chuckle deep in the night,
Every sigh is a comedic beat,
Creating a symphony soft and sweet.

In each moment, joy's embrace we find,
A melody of hearts intertwined,
In the warmth of every breath we share,
Laughter reigns upon us like fresh air.

The Dwelling of Brave Aspirations

In a house of dreams we play,
Where hopes and laughs come out to play.
A cat with shades, a dog in shoes,
They dance around, they play to lose.

A fridge that talks, it tells a joke,
The steaming kettle starts to poke.
With flying beans and popcorn skies,
We giggle as we munch and sigh.

The toaster's winks, the blender sings,
A joyful tune of silly things.
The walls are painted with our smiles,
The floor is paved with laughter miles.

So here we dwell on wobbly chairs,
Inventing whims without a care.
In this odd place where dreams are bright,
Every mistake is pure delight.

The Songbird's Lament of Tomorrow

Oh little bird, you sing so true,
With melodies of mischief too.
You chirp of bread and lost shoe laces,
Your tunes bring joy to all the faces.

A worm will laugh and strut with pride,
As you lament your clumsy glide.
But even when you crash and flop,
You rise again—oh never stop!

Tomorrow's song is yet to chime,
With giggles, hiccups, and silly rhyme.
The skies may frown, the clouds may sigh,
Yet you continue to tickle the sky.

So flap your wings and spin around,
In your own world of silly sound.
With every note you give a wink,
In laughter's glow, we pause and think.

Whispers of the Everlasting Sky

The clouds conspire, with giggles loud,
They're plotting mischief, whimsical shroud.
A raindrop slips, gives way to play,
As puddles scatter laughter's way.

The stars at midnight wink and glow,
As if they've seen our little show.
A comet's tail is wrapped in glee,
"Come join us now, just let it be!"

With whispers soft, the winds cavort,
As nature plays in a silly sport.
They jest and tease, they twirl about,
In skies of dreams, they laugh and shout.

So let us dance in moonlit streams,
Where life is filled with tangled dreams.
Under the whims of cosmic jest,
We'll find our joy and laugh the best.

Where Dreams Collide with Reality

In a realm where wishes flip and flop,
A purple elephant strolls, then hops.
He juggles stars, and laughs so grand,
While jelly beans dance hand in hand.

Reality sneezes, dreams take flight,
A bicycle rides up to the night.
With every turn, absurdity reigns,
As whirling thoughts race through our brains.

We tiptoe on clouds made of cream,
And sip our coffee from a dream.
The laws of gravity seem to bend,
In this world where humor is a trend.

So here we stand, both bold and shy,
With silly thoughts that zip and fly.
In this grand place where nothing's wrong,
We live and laugh; let's sing our song.

Shelter from the Storm of Doubt

When clouds parade and rain does jeer,
We sit inside with snacks and cheer.
The world outside may frown and pout,
But we're just fine in here, no doubt!

The cat's a captain, on her throne,
She claims the couch; that's her alone.
We argue who will fetch the tea,
Yet laugh till stomachs ache, you see.

The wind may howl, but we're all grand,
With silly games by chance planned.
Our fortress built with jokes and puns,
In every laugh, the doubt just runs.

In the Embrace of Infinite Possibilities

A world of choices, oh so vast,
We ponder pizza, tacos, cast!
Should we explore or just play games?
Oh wait, what's for dinner? Who's to blame?

Each path we pick, a goofy dance,
Sometimes we trip, it's just our chance.
With every fall, we laugh, then stand,
Shenanigans, our sweet life's brand.

The mirror's cracked, our hair's a fright,
But who's to care? We're out tonight!
In every wobble, we find our way,
In silly tales, our hearts will play.

The Echoing Cheers of Tomorrow

Tomorrow calls with all its flair,
But first, let's finish this comfy chair.
With popcorn bowls and laughter loud,
We cheer for dreams, both bold and proud.

The ghosts of plans that didn't soar,
Now play the cast on our living floor.
A dance-off here with socks that slip,
Tomorrow, oh what a funny trip!

We're crafting futures, one giggle at a time,
With every slip-up, we create a rhyme.
So raise a toast with fizzy drinks,
To all our hopes and silly winks!

A Hearth of Gentle Resilience

In a cozy corner, laughter spins,
As we juggle chores and all life's whims.
The cat's our judge in this wacky game,
She rolls her eyes, but we'll never tame.

A burnt dinner? Oh, what a scene!
The smoke alarms play our favorite theme.
But with a wink and a silly toast,
We feast on snacks, we love the most!

With stories shared and hearts held high,
We face the chaos, laugh till we cry.
In this soft glow, we find our heat,
A family's bond, oh so sweet!

The Lanterns of Tomorrow's Dawn

Under skies that giggle bright,
We chase shadows, silly sight.
A lantern winks, 'Don't be so crass!'
'Just catch some joy, let good times pass!'

With laughter gleaming in our eyes,
Each dawn reveals another prize.
We stumble, trip, on dreams we find,
A dance of wits, oh so unrefined!

Each lantern's glow, a happy tease,
Lighting paths like buzzing bees.
We skip and hop, like kids in play,
Who knew hope could be this gay?

With giggles loud and hearts on fire,
Each moment sparks with pure desire.
So grab your hat and join the fun,
Tomorrow's dawn has just begun!

Embracing the Winds of Change

A gust arrives, we squeal and shout,
As hats take flight, there's no doubt.
We twirl and sway like dandelion,
In winds that tease, we feel so fine!

Jumping puddles, splashing wide,
With each new breeze, we cast aside.
The world's a stage, our dance the play,
Why let the winds blow us away?

With every whirl, we chase the fun,
Clinging tight, hearts come undone.
The skies may frown, but we just grin,
For changes spark the thrill within!

As we embrace what comes our way,
We laugh and leap, come what may.
So bring on storms, let's ride the wave,
In crazy winds, we'll learn to brave!

In the Sanctuary of Longing

In corners dark, where dreams do dwell,
Whispers of wishes weave a spell.
A cat's meow or a dog's soft bark,
We ponder longings in the dark.

With every sigh, a joke we share,
In hopes and wishes, we find the rare.
Does a wish get lost in the fridge?
Or does it dance like a squirrel on a bridge?

So here's to hearts that brave the quest,
With humor wrapped in a cozy nest.
Longing's a friend with a silly grin,
Invite him in, let the fun begin!

Let's dream aloud, make wishes loud,
In a sanctuary where we're funny and proud.
Together we laugh, together we sigh,
In this quirky place, let's always fly!

The Tapestry of Unwritten Journeys

With threads of laughter, bright and bold,
We weave a tale, a sight to behold.
Stitching dreams with a cheeky twist,
Who knew journeys could be so blissed?

Each step we take, a dance of grace,
As we write our paths at a whimsical pace.
Did you see that mushroom cap?
It waved at me, and I took a nap!

The tapestry grows with every twist,
With mischief and joy, none can resist.
What tale is next? With giggles, we plot,
Each adventure awaits, give it a shot!

As we thread these tales with glee,
Life's funniest moments are the key.
So grab your needle, let's have some fun,
Unwritten dreams shine like the sun!

The Garden of Resilience

In a patch where laughter grows,
We plant our dreams like little crows.
With seeds of joy and water's grace,
We dance around in a funny race.

We prune our fears with garden shears,
And laugh away the silliest tears.
The weeds of doubt may sometimes sprout,
But our laughter's what it's all about.

We grow tall sunflowers, bright and bold,
Trading stories, so funny, retold.
With gnomes that giggle and fairies sing,
We find the joy that gardening brings.

So here's to the blooms, both wild and neat,
In our quirky patch, life's joys repeat.
With every chuckle, our spirits fly,
In the garden where laughter is the sky.

Underneath the Veil of Faith

In shadows where the giggles creep,
We find our dreams in a jolly heap.
With faith that winks and whispers bright,
We trade our worries for pure delight.

The treasure maps are written in jest,
With dotted lines to our funny quest.
We stumble through with the lightest heart,
In a comedy show, we each play a part.

With faith like sand in a clumsy hand,
We build our castles upon soft land.
And if they tumble, we burst with glee,
For every failure's a victory spree.

So let's toast to the joy, with chiffon dreams,
Under wraps of laughter, or so it seems.
In the veil of faith where we all belong,
We sing our silliness as life's sweet song.

Threads of Anticipation

With threads of gold, we weave our day,
Anticipation is here to play.
We stitch up hope with a needle's grin,
And laugh at the messes our dreams get in.

Each fabric swatch holds a funny tale,
Of failed attempts and ships that sail.
With patterns bold, we sally forth,
Sewing the quirks of silly worth.

The tapestry of laughter's spun,
In colors bright, we have such fun.
With every loop, a giggle's curled,
In this stitched-up map of our funny world.

So here's to the threads, vibrant and wild,
In anticipation's lap, we're all a child.
With laughter sewn in every seam,
We'll wear our joy as the grandest theme.

A Haven Where Wishes Bloom

In a pairing of dreams, the wishes jive,
Dancing around in a joyful hive.
With petals of giggles and stems of cheer,
We cultivate joy, year after year.

Our garden of wishes is quite the sight,
With sparkling hopes, all sunny and bright.
We water the laughter, we prune the fears,
A bouquet of giggles, through all the years.

With butterflies that tell jokes in flight,
And ladybugs wearing bow ties just right,
In this haven where dreams get to bloom,
Our imaginations find plenty of room.

So let's spread our wishes, bloom them wide,
In this silly garden, let laughter reside.
With every chuckle that floats through the air,
We'll make wishes blossom, beyond compare.

In the Embrace of Solace

In a cozy corner with a shoe,
A sock with a hole, its partner too.
They huddle together, all torn and worn,
Laughing at laundry that looks forlorn.

A cat thinks it's magic, a swirling spree,
While the couch cushions giggle in glee.
Coffee spills secrets, and crumbs share tales,
While the clock winks, ignoring our fails.

The fridge hums a tune, a dizzying sound,
As vegetables dance and peas leap around.
In this strange room, where chaos reigns,
We find joy in the wildest of gains.

So let's toast to the mess, the chaos, the cheer,
With mismatched socks and leftover beer.
In laughter we dwell; it's the ultimate scope,
In the silliness hidden, we find our hope.

Threads of Faith in the Tapestry of Time

Grandma's old quilt, full of patches,
Each square a story, joy mixes with hatches.
A patch of blue jeans, a slice of red flair,
With stitching so crooked, it shows we care.

It covers the couch like a big warm hug,
But cat claws attack it, a mischievous bug.
Each stitch a battle, a snip and a fray,
Yet, it keeps our warmth, come what may.

The threads all whisper, "We're a bit shoddy,"
Yet they keep us cozy, all calm and gaudy.
As we sit in delight, with popcorn to share,
Life's tapestry shines in the oddest of wear.

So let's cherish the quirks and each little hole,
For they add to our charm; they make us whole.
In the fabric of laughter, let our hearts chime,
Woven so tightly, through the fabric of time.

When Wishes Dance on Moonlit Waters

On a pond so silly, where frogs take the lead,
They leap and they croak, like a wild dancing creed.
The moon grins down with a twinkling tune,
While fish chuckle softly, beneath the balloons.

Stars throw confetti like they're at a ball,
As squirrels in tuxedos seem ready to call.
Wishes float gently on lily pads wide,
While turtles play tag in their slow-motion glide.

A wish whispered loudly, "I want extra cheese!"
And the owls just hoot, "We prefer the trees!"
But this silly soirée on shimmering tides,
Holds dreams wrapped in laughter, where nonsense abides.

So let's join the frolic on switched-up delights,
With frogs, and a wish, and perhaps some light bites.
For beneath the moon's laughter, we find our cheer,
In a pond of wishes, our joy's crystal clear.

The Horizon of Infinite Possibilities

A bike with a wheel that's slightly wonky,
Takes me on journeys that feel just funky.
With each wobbly turn, I'm sailing through air,
In the land of unknown, I show no care.

Clouds race above like kittens in play,
They peek at me, giggling all the way.
The grass clumps together, having its chat,
While I straddle the silliness of my old hat.

Each path is a riddle, each stone has a jest,
As squirrels throw comedy, putting me to test.
Perhaps I might find a rainbow today,
Or trip on a thought that lights up the way.

With shoes untied, and a spirit so light,
I'm ready for mischief, come day or night.
So let's chase the sun, and who knows what's near,
In the horizon of laughter, we'll conquer our fear.

In Search of Dawn's Promise

I woke up late; the sun's a tease,
My toast is burnt, my coffee's freeze.
I chase the light with silly shoes,
A morning dance, I've got the moves.

The cat's my judge, she won't let go,
She thinks I'm nuts, but I don't know.
Yet giggles spill like morning dew,
I search for dawn with laughs anew.

A bird on branch sings off-key tune,
Each note a word, like someone's spoon.
I bob my head, and sing along,
A morning farce, our happy song.

So if you find the dawn unsure,
Just peek inside and find the cure.
With laughter bright and silly cheer,
The day will start with joyful gear.

Shelter from the Storm of Doubt

I built a fort from couch and sheets,
Inside I laugh; outside, it beats.
The thunder roars, but I won't fuss,
I've sandwiches and juice; what a plus!

In my kingdom of fluffy dreams,
A jester's hat, or so it seems.
My teddy bears all form a band,
Their giggles echo, oh so grand.

Outside's a tempest, rain like cake,
A sprinkle here, a puddle quake.
But in my fortress, I reign supreme,
With laughter as my trusty theme.

So storms may come with winds that frown,
But snacks and jokes won't let me down.
I wrap my thoughts in humor's cloak,
In my merry world, I smile and stoke.

A Canvas of Resilience

I paint my day with splops of fun,
A brilliant mess; does life weigh a ton?
With purple skies and polka dot trees,
Each brush a giggle, each stroke a tease.

My canvas sings with colors bright,
A masterpiece of silly plight.
With every drip, I dance and sway,
Embracing joy, come what may.

I spill my paint; my cat jumps high,
She lands in red, oh my, oh my!
Yet laughter's swirl can mend a wall,
A happy heart can conquer all.

So grab your brushes, let's create,
A world where whims and giggles wait.
With vibrant hues 'neath sunny beams,
We'll paint our lives with crazy dreams.

Beneath the Silent Guard of Starlit Skies

As stars pop out like bubble gum,
I lie on grass, my thoughts a hum.
A shoot of light, a comet's race,
I giggle loud in nature's space.

The moon's my buddy, all aglow,
We share the secrets that we know.
He's whispers soft: 'Don't take it slow,'
I wink back, 'Time flies, just so!'

The night is young; we'll make it wild,
With silly games, like laughter's child.
I chase my dreams like fireflies,
And catch a laugh that never dies.

So here's a toast to nights so bright,
Where whimsy dances, hearts take flight.
With every twinkle, dreams arise,
As joy ignites beneath the skies.

Navigating a Sea of Dreams

In a boat made of marshmallows,
Sailing on soda pop streams,
I row with a spoon, oh dear me,
With jellyfish wearing bright gleams.

Paddling past clouds shaped like pies,
Each wave is a tickle, I grin,
Coconut dolphins splash with cheer,
While gummy bears dive and swim.

My compass spins wildly, it's true,
It points to a land made of cake,
Where laughter's a treasure to find,
And everyone dances, awake.

As we drift into night's sugary bliss,
The stars are just sprinkles above,
I chuckle at whimsies galore,
In this sea of dreams filled with love.

The Garden where Futures Flourish

In a garden of socks and old shoes,
The daisies wear hats made of cheese,
We water the weeds with sweet lemonade,
And laugh at the wind as it sneezes.

The carrots all dance with a jig,
While the tomatoes gossip a lot,
"I saw a squirrel wearing a tie!"
"Oh hush, that's just Bob in a spot!"

Sunflowers keep track of the time,
With faces that spin and do twists,
They whisper their secrets to bees,
And the butterflies write 'Top Ten Lists.'

Here futures grow wild with delight,
In a patch where the oddities bloom,
We pluck at the dreams like ripe fruit,
Each one smells like freshly baked gloom!

A Glimpse of Light in the Gloom

In a world where the shadows wear hats,
And giggle at squirrels in the rain,
I skip through puddles of chocolate milk,
Laughing at my own silly train.

A glowworm guides me with grace,
As I dance with the mice in the moon,
Their tiny feet tap out a beat,
And the evening hums a bright tune.

Monsters hide under beds, or so we say,
But they all play cards with great flair,
And joke about their terrible breath,
While we munch on popcorn and stare.

So here, amidst the invisible cheer,
I find light where the humor gleams,
In glimpses of laughter we share,
We weave our most whimsical dreams.

The Cradle of Whispered Hopes

In a cradle made out of gumdrops,
We rock to the beat of the breeze,
While dreams hang like brightly colored lights,
Dripping sweet thoughts with great ease.

Giggles float up like balloons,
And tickles are served on a tray,
In a land where the wishes all giggle,
They prank the stars every day.

Puppies talk business with clouds,
As squirrels barter nuts with no shame,
Each whisper a secret, a giggle,
In this playground where none is the same.

So let's cradle our hopes with a smirk,
In this whimsical world of delight,
Where laughter wraps 'round like a blanket,
And silly dreams dance through the night.

Dawn's Arrival at the Edge of Despair

As the sun peeks over shadows long,
The coffee brews, it hums a song.
Birds start chirping, a silly cheer,
Who knew despair could disappear?

Pajamas worn, like armor tight,
Do I look good? Oh, not tonight!
Yet with a wink and a stretch, I say,
Let's face the world in our own way.

The toast is burnt, and so's the bread,
But laughter sizzles in our head.
Together we dance, through trials we leap,
In the land where even dreams can sleep.

So raise your cup, let laughter flow,
We'll mock our troubles, give them a show.
For at dawn's edge, with humor piqued,
We'll craft the joy that we now seek.

In the Halls of Infinite Belief

In halls adorned with silly dreams,
Jokes echo louder than it seems.
With every step, a giggle spills,
We chase the light, defy the chills.

The walls hold stories, wild and vague,
Of cat-wearing hats and dancing snakes.
We'll dare to question, with a grin,
What fun awaits? Let's just dive in!

With every corner, a surprise awaits,
A joke, a pun, as laughter rates.
So grab a friend, and don't be shy,
In here, we soar, like clouds on high.

The clock might tick, but time's a joke,
We'll giggle 'til our sides provoke.
In these halls, our spirits thrive,
Where laughter reigns, we're most alive.

Raindrops of Change on Parched Soil

A drizzle starts, a pitter-pat,
On rooftops where the squirrels chat.
We laugh as puddles form below,
With every drop, we steal the show.

The plants rejoice, they dance around,
While ants parade, they run aground.
With raincoats on, we stomp so bold,
In moods like this, we break the mold.

Each raindrop carries a wacky tale,
Of silly fish in a comic gale.
We splash through life, no care in sight,
So let it rain, we'll be alright!

With every storm, a giggle grows,
Watered dreams bloom in soft repose.
So let it pour, come join the fun,
In this wet world, we've already won!

The Flame that Ignites the Dark

In shadows deep, a flicker bright,
A candle dances, a comical sight.
It wobbles and sways, like a puppy's prance,
Inviting us all for a goofy dance.

As stories whisper from cornered nooks,
They skip and loop like pesky books.
With laughter sparked, we gather near,
To roast marshmallows, oh so dear.

The shadows chuckle, they join the play,
With flickering jokes that brighten the day.
In the glow, we share our quirks,
For here, even darkness works.

So let the flame, our laughter weave,
Brightening minds, we won't deceive.
In this cozy space, we'll find our way,
With humor's light, we're here to stay.

The Heart's Refuge of Untamed Courage

In a closet that shouts with sass,
A superhero cape made of glass.
With a tin can phone that rings so bright,
I share my secrets on a taco night.

Worms doing yoga, they twist and bend,
While my cat gives lectures, think she'll attend?
A dance party starts with a jar of jam,
While the goldfish dreams of becoming a ham.

Dreams do a tango with laughter and cheer,
Pants on a chandelier, what a sight here!
In the refuge of giggles, we're never shy,
With peanut butter toast flying by.

So lift your tea cup, come join the fun,
In a whirl of laughter, our race has begun.
With a bubble of joy that refuses to pop,
We make our own courage, we never will stop.

Gardens of Belief in a Concrete Jungle

In pots of dreams, plants sprout and grow,
With daisies arguing on where to go.
A sunflower's gossip, tall and proud,
While daisies in dilemma whisper aloud.

Bees wearing glasses, discussing the heat,
While ants throw a party with crumbs as a feast.
Concrete walls frown but petals still dance,
In this crazy patch, we take our chance.

A carrot in therapy, sharing its strife,
Claiming it longs for a more lively life.
While broccoli's plans of escape go awry,
As stalks do their best just to reach for the sky.

With laughter dressed up in pure silly cheer,
In our jungle of dreams, there's nothing to fear.
So come take a stroll, look at what's spry,
In gardens of belief, we reach for the sky.

Illuminating the Path Unknown

With a flashlight made out of marshmallow fluff,
We stumble along, but it's never too tough.
Glowworms are giggling, lighting the track,
While shadows do their best to hold us back.

A compass that spins in circles so wide,
Points to the ice cream shop, what a ride!
Footsteps of penguins join in our quest,
As we wander through laughter, we're truly blessed.

Frogs with monocles ponder our fate,
They croak out a riddle about a big plate.
With each step we take, a chuckle we find,
In the path of the unknown, hilarity's blind.

So fear not the journey, take off that frown,
It's an adventure, and we're in this town.
With every wild turn, let your spirit be free,
For there's magic afoot, just wait and see.

The Alchemy of Hope and Time

In a cauldron of giggles, we stir and we shake,
With jellybeans dancing for magic's sake.
A splash of good fortune, a pinch of delight,
Turned bananas into laughter, oh what a sight!

Time wears a hat made of rainbow sprinkles,
With clock hands that tickle, oh how it twinkles!
We mix up our worries with whipped cream and cheer,
And watch as they vanish like socks in a sphere.

In the alchemy bubbling, we find our spice,
Marshmallow moments, we'll add them twice.
Cinnamon whispers blend with old dreams,
Transforming our troubles into laughter's beams.

So gather around for this feast of the mind,
In the recipe of joy, let's leave doubts behind.
With every oddities, let's celebrate time,
In the alchemy of life, all things will align.

The Gateway to Tomorrow's Embrace

A little door swings wide with cheer,
Where dreams come in with cookies near.
Whiskers twitch and kittens play,
Laughing loud, it's a sunny day.

A dance of socks upon the floor,
A cat that steals the cake from yore.
With every giggle, hope does bloom,
As we sweep up crumbs, our hearts consume.

Of peanut butter and jelly fights,
With balloons that fill the starry nights.
We paint the walls with shades of glee,
Where laughter echoes, wild and free.

So here we stand, our hearts entwined,
In silly hats and ice cream dined.
For every jest, a chuckle grows,
Tomorrow's joy, as sunshine flows.

Where Breezes Carry Hopes Anew

The winds of change bring silly news,
Of dancing squirrels in funny shoes.
They pirouette on branches high,
While giggles float and laughter flies.

Old fences creak and sway about,
While cows all moo, and goats just shout.
We chase our dreams on skateboard wheels,
With dreams that burst like jelly peels.

Underneath the rainbow's arc,
We spot a frog that sings a lark.
With the breeze behind, we spin and dive,
In silly games, we feel alive.

So let the breezes carry light,
To tickle toes and inspire delight.
For hope is found in every jest,
In laughter's arms, we feel the best.

Parables of the Unseen Wonder

In the pantry hides a wizard's cup,
With secrets brewed to lift us up.
Each sip a tale of silly pranks,
Where giggles echo in friendship ranks.

The socks that vanish, the shoes that dance,
In this jolly world, we take our chance.
A parable told in buttered toast,
It's mornings like this that we love most.

The spoons all sing, the forks all play,
While butterflies laugh, come what may.
In unseen wonders, joy unfolds,
With whispers of hope, our laughter holds.

So gather round for stories bright,
In the space where whimsy takes flight.
For every tale, a giggle ignites,
In the magic we find in silly sights.

Tides of Change under the Canvas of Night

As stars begin their nightly grace,
The waves come in a laughing race.
With moonlit splashes and winks all round,
We build our castles on sandy ground.

Seagulls squawk like they've won a prize,
In a world where silly never dies.
The moon hides jokes in silver beams,
And tickles the sea with dreams and schemes.

Tides come high, and then they sway,
In rhythm with our night-time play.
We splash and fall in merriment,
As candles drizzle—sweet content.

So dance with waves and giggle bright,
For hope is found in every night.
In tides of change, we find our way,
With laughter charting our next play.

The Canvas of Dreamcatchers

Upon a canvas bright and wide,
Dreamcatchers dance and play inside.
They catch the dreams that wander free,
And make a quilt of joy, you see.

A spider's silk is what they claim,
To catch the dreams—a funny game.
With feathers tickling all around,
They laugh at snoring, oh what sound!

Each night they weave a tale unique,
Of heroes bold and cacti chic.
They paint the skies in colors bold,
And sell them off for silver and gold.

So swing beneath their gleeful eye,
And dream of pancakes stacked up high.
For in this canvas, dreams don't stop,
Just watch out for that candy shop!

Reflections in the Ripple of Time

In puddles deep, reflections prance,
Time takes a wiggle, joins the dance.
With every splash, a fish does grin,
As seconds tick, they wiggle in.

The clock strikes twelve, a cat won't meow,
Instead, it sings a rabbit's vow.
So laughter flows, like water's play,
In ripples funny throughout the day.

A duck in waders, oh what a sight,
Splashes around, dancing in light.
While turtles giggle, roll through the muck,
An orchestra of joy, just pure luck!

With every ripple, a story grows,
Of winking fairies and garden gnomes.
So dive right in, let laughter chime,
In these wild reflections of time!

Under the Arch of Intent

Under an arch made of old cheese,
Intentions twist like the autumn breeze.
With every thought, a squirrel takes flight,
Flipping through futures, what a sight!

A trampoline of dreams to explore,
Each jump a giggle, who could ask for more?
While intentions race, with legs of spaghetti,
Their dance tires the toes, not the confetti!

Goblin snacks are scattered about,
In the arch of intent, they scream and shout.
With every nibble, a laugh erupts,
As intentions tumble and bubble up!

So join the fun, make a wish on a dime,
Under this arch, where life feels sublime.
Let your laughter rise, no room for lament,
For here we gather with light hearts, content!

The Pathway to Uncharted Realms

On a pathway paved with jelly beans,
We journey forth to laugh extreme.
With minty trees and chocolate streams,
We navigate through silly dreams.

A bear in a bow tie leads the way,
Telling jokes that brighten the day.
The map unfolds, with crayons bright,
As laughter echoes, taking flight.

Through fields of giggles and tickle grass,
We hop along, letting worries pass.
With each step forward, joy expands,
In realms unseen, with silly bands.

So join us now, be silly, be free,
On pathways where joy is the only decree.
Adventure awaits in the strangest forms,
With laughter galore, where fun truly warms!

Chronicles of a Hopeful Heart

In a land where dreams trip and fall,
A hopeful heart stands proud and tall.
It wears mismatched socks, a goofy grin,
Believing it can't help but win.

Every misstep is a dance, oh yes!
With jellybeans in hand, who could guess?
It jumps through puddles, makes a splash,
Skipping along, no need for cash!

When clouds roll in like a giant cat,
It takes out its umbrella, just like that!
It twirls and sways, it won't give in,
Laughing at life, with a cheeky spin.

With a heart of bacon and dreams of cheese,
Our hopeful hero rolls with ease.
In this quirky quest, the skies aren't gray,
For laughter's the tune on this wacky day.

Embers from the Ashes of Yesterday

Yesterday's troubles are toasting marshmallows,
As sparks of laughter dance like gallows.
From ash to giggles, we find our light,
With every chuckle, we take to flight.

In a smoky haze, we find our cheer,
Through the flames, a joke appears.
"Why did the scarecrow win an award?"
Because he was outstanding, that's not ignored!

We gather our woes, like dusty old socks,
Turning them into spectacular frocks.
Dust off the laughter, sprinkle it wide,
In the ashes of yesterday, joy takes stride.

With each ember shining, we toast to our fate,
For in the end, it's laughter that's great.
So let's gather 'round and share a jest,
For humor's the compass to life's lively quest.

The Sanctuary of What Could Be

In a whimsical haven where wishes jump,
Where kittens play chess and pigs do the thump.
Hope wears a tutu and dances in style,
While rainbows giggle and dreams stretch a mile.

Imagine a place where pizza can sing,
Where socks hold hands, and jellybeans fling.
With marshmallow clouds and laughter's embrace,
It's a sanctuary full of silly grace.

Maybe today's troubles float in a boat,
With silly giraffes wearing hats that gloat.
We'll sail on the tides of what could be,
And share our weirdness, just you and me.

So pull up a chair, let's giggle unplanned,
In this joyful space, where life is unplanned.
With whimsy and hope, let's lark and roam,
For this quirky sanctuary feels like home.

Fantasies Entwined in Reality

In dreams where unicorns ride on cars,
And reality giggles, wearing silly scars.
We chase the stars and high-five the moon,
While dancing with shadows, we find our tune.

Backwards we walk, on stilts made of gummy,
As our laughter echoes, a pleasant dummy.
Wishing wells are just puddles in disguise,
Where fish wear hats and tell us lies.

The sandwich sings its own funky song,
As we twirl 'round the kitchen, nothing feels wrong.
In this tangled tale, we dip and dive,
For the fancier side of life is alive!

So let's weave our fantasies into the now,
With silly aspirations and a laughter vow.
Reality's charm, oh what a delight,
As we dream big and dance through the night.

The Tapestry of Unwritten Tomorrow

In a world where socks always mismatch,
Dreams dance like noodles in a big pot,
Tomorrow's tangle is hard to detach,
Yet laughter's the thread that ties up the knot.

Jellybeans drop from the clouds like rain,
Pigeons wear hats and honk for a fate,
We chase our own tails in a joyful train,
Making plans that don't want to wait.

The sun takes a selfie, all smiles and rays,
While chairs throw a party just for the cat,
Time spins in circles, it frolics and plays,
And life is a game, stop worrying 'bout that!

When yesterday's whispers get caught in a breeze,
We build giant castles with marshmallow cream,
The future's a puzzle that giggles and sneezes,
Each piece a grin, a whimsical dream.

Shadows That Speak to the Heart

Silhouettes dance on the walls of my mind,
Whispering secrets in a language of sass,
They giggle and squawk, they're one of a kind,
Telling tales of future, a whimsical class.

With glasses of lemonade, they toast to the sky,
While shadows play hopscotch on the floor of my dreams,
Together we laugh, and oh how we fly,
In a comedy reel full of whims and themes.

Each corner we bend steals the light with a grin,
Those shadows remind us not to take it so tough,
In every adventure, the fun's buried within,
And amidst all the chaos, we learn to be rough.

So here's to the echoes that linger in air,
They promise to hold us when days seem askew,
Together we'll giggle, we'll boldly declare,
That merriment grows when in shadow we strew.

Whispers of Change Across the Landscape

Listen closely, the daisies are laughing,
They munch on the sun with a twist of delight,
While trees trade their leaves, the breeze is drafting,
Plans for a party that lasts through the night.

The clouds pull a prank, they tickle the rain,
As puddles reflect the wild ballet of springs,
In this circus of colors, we'll dance through the pain,
With jesters and dreams, oh the joy that it brings!

Grasshoppers croon in a jazzy refrain,
While owls crack jokes, wearing glasses of style,
The world spins around in a whimsical chain,
Where change sounds like laughter that stretches a mile.

So sing with the flowers, let laughter take wing,
Each moment a puzzle, each twist a delight,
In this landscape of smiles, we'll dance and we'll swing,
And find joy in the whispers that dance in the light.

The Blossoming of Unseen Journeys

A snail on a quest, oh what fun!
Its house packed light, a roof on the run.
It dreams of adventures, near and far,
While strangers just laugh at its shiny car.

Each step is a giggle, a twist and a swirl,
With every slow inch, it gives life a twirl.
A compass of laughter, its guide in the night,
With friends made of moss, it journeys with delight.

The flowers shout jokes, the trees sing along,
The wind whispers puns, all silly and strong.
With each slime trail left in the damp, cool earth,
The path is a playground, a land full of mirth.

Oh, how it enjoys this slippery ride,
A marathon of giggles with friends by its side.
So here's to the snails, and their journeys en route,
With laughter as luggage, they're ready to scoot!

Conversations with the Universe

I asked the stars about my old sock,
They chuckled and winked, 'It's lost in the flock!'
The moon just chuckled, 'You know the tale,
It's probably off sailing, or chasing a whale.'

'But where does the sun find its endless glow?'
The cosmos replied, 'In the warmth of a show!'
And there in the silence, a comet flew by,
With a wink and a nudge, it carried a pie.

Dinosaurs giggled from their distant past,
'We lost our last game of hide and seek fast!'
The universe laughed, 'Life is just grand,
Even socks with adventures might get out of hand.'

So I sit and I ponder, with stars for my guides,
While giggles and whispers are what the night hides.
In conversations like these, I find it's a joy,
To banter with galaxies, oh what a ploy!

The Weaving of Collective Aspirations

Once, threads of laughter tangled in glee,
They plotted a quilt for the world to see.
With colors of dreams and patterns of fun,
They stitched up a plan 'til it shone like the sun.

The weavers convened in a garden of cheer,
'Let's make something special, something sincere.'
With scissors of joy and fabric of hope,
They fashioned a blanket, a whimsical slope.

Each patch told a story, each knot made it real,
Of wishes unspoken, all woven with zeal.
Then a cat sneezed stripes that got mixed in the game,
And suddenly laughter erupted, quite lame!

But laughter's the thread that held it all tight,
A reminder that life could be colorful light.
So here's to the weavers with dreams intertwined,
Creating a tapestry for all humankind!

Stargazing in the Shade of Tomorrow

With sunglasses on, I looked at the stars,
'Why do they twinkle? Are they driving cars?'
A friend by my side said, 'Nah, they just play,
In a cosmic pool where they splash every day.'

We spread out a blanket, prepared for a chat,
Then sat up quite straight when we spotted a cat.
The feline was pondering beneath glowing skies,
'Should I chase those bright lights or take a nap? Yikes!'

Amid giggles and lore, the night hummed along,
With jokes from the planets—our favorite song.
We dreamed up the wonders that tomorrow could hold,
While dodging the giggles and tales that unfold.

With a wink from the universe, dreams took their flight,
We laughed 'til it tickled, a magical night.
In the shade of tomorrow, with starlit delight,
We planned our next adventure for laughter's invite!

Silhouettes of Courage in a Storm

A cat in a raincoat, oh what a sight,
Strutting through puddles, quite full of delight.
Umbrellas like mushrooms, all over the street,
Dodging the raindrops, escaping defeat.

A dog in galoshes, pathos at play,
Sliding on sidewalks, what a clumsy ballet.
Laughter erupts, splashes in tow,
Even the storm can't dim the show.

The trees dance around, twirling in glee,
While squirrels think they're all acrobats from sea.
Rhythm of thunder plays a wild tune,
As courage leaps high like a cartoon.

So when clouds come rolling, don't hide or despair,
Join the parade, with joy to declare.
With laughter and whimsy, we'll weather the gale,
In the storm's silly heart, we shall prevail.

Mythical Seeds of Transformation

A seed fell one day, with dreams in its mind,
Wishing to sprout, but oh, it was blind.
It dreamed of a cactus, but grew a bouquet,
Just goes to show dreams can go astray.

A snail held a conference, all in a rush,
Planning their futures, in quite a hush.
They plotted the garden, each hoping to shine,
Except for one fellow, who just wanted wine.

The bees wore monocles, sipping on tea,
Debating the merits of flowers, quite free.
In their buzzing debate, the petals took flight,
Transforming the garden to a colorful sight.

With laughter and giggles from all around,
Their mythical tales of growth know no bound.
So plant your odd seeds, let them laugh or cry,
For in jest and folly, transformations can fly.

The Pulse of Hope Through Endless Time

Tick-tock went the clock, with a wink and a grin,
Spouting wise wisdom as the day would begin.
With a dance on the hour, it claimed quite the fame,
As people would chuckle, they'd all know its name.

A tortoise named Larry raced past, oh so slow,
Claiming he'd win, 'cause it's all just for show.
With a wink at the hare, who raced far too fast,
In a twist of the fate, all fell out of contrast.

The future's a jester, with tricks up its sleeve,
Making challenges comical, easy to believe.
So let's raise a toast to the quirks of old time,
Where hope winks and jesters bring laughter in rhyme.

In this circus of life, embrace each new chance,
With a giggle and tickle, join the wild dance.
For hope's not a whisper, but a jubilant shout,
As time spins the tales of the brave and the stout.

Breathing Life into Forgotten Dreams

There once was a dream, lost under the bed,
With dust bunnies dancing, in party hats red.
It laughed at the chaos, said, 'Let's go outside!'
As it hopped on a broomstick, refusing to hide.

A sock with a story, missing its mate,
Fluffed up with courage, decided to skate.
Around the corner, it zoomed with flair,
Only to spiral and land in the air!

An old shoe lamented, 'Oh, where have you been?'
While memories jingled like sweet tambourines.
This silliness bloomed, with each twist and turn,
As dreams once forgotten began to return.

So gather your whims, let them twirl in the breeze,
For life's too amusing to take with unease.
With laughter as fuel, let dreams take to flight,
And breathe every moment—oh, what a delight!

www.ingramcontent.com/pod-product-compliance
Lightning Source LLC
Chambersburg PA
CBHW062110280426
43661CB00086B/439